Pedro's Project

Aurora Martorell

Illustrator: Pedro Penizotto

Richmond PUBLISHING

3

It's time for the football match. Pedro is sad.

Pedro plays very well, but Luke's team doesn't. Luke is angry.

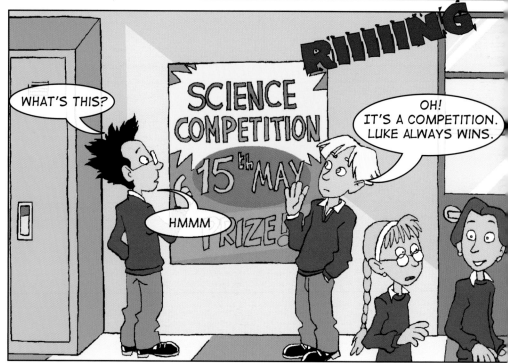

6

7

9

10

11

 13

 15

month later...

The next day…

It's time for everyone to show their projects.

Pedro and his friends run to the kitchen.

Everyone is in the dining hall.

Picture Dictionary

British

cut down

danger

dining hall

experiment

football match

gardener

hide

pot

rainforest

scientist

team

 24